Quilting for Beginners

Table of Contents

Introduction

Chapter One

The History of Quilting - Hawaii, the United Kingdom, South Africa, Australia and the United States of America

Chapter Two

The Technical Bits

Chapter Three

Quilt Styles and Decorating

Chapter Four

Unique and Important Quilts Across the World

Chapter Five

Births, Marriages and Deaths

Conclusion

Introduction

Quilting is as old as the hills, and for many, has that wonderful combination of domestic necessity, social cohesion, and craftwork and commemoration.

Quilting methods don't vary enormously throughout the world, but the designs are largely specific to a country, or a society, although the traditional American patchwork designs have become loved world wide.

It is wonderful to have such a craft, which is a means of handing down traditions amongst womenfolk mainly, and which has an end product that can both look beautiful, and keep you warm at night.

An exception to this is of course the Hawaiian quilting tradition, which began under the tutelage of the missionaries, and evolved into a means of recording the Hawaiian beliefs and lives. Their quilts talk of their gods, their departed spirits, the new members of their society yet to be born, and the main historical and cultural events of their society. Their use of the beautiful flowers and the love of their culture give Hawaiian quilting a truly magical and precious quality.

In colder climates, the quilting circle was an opportunity for the women to come together, to talk over the major matters of the day and to provide invaluable support for each other.

The new settlers in The United States of America were hardy and tough. Most of them had to start from scratch. Homes had to be built, and furnished, and in these days, nearly everything had to be grown or made.

Needlework was a very necessary skill for a woman. Without this, they would not be able to make their clothes, and would not be able to make the soft furnishings that not only 'make a house into a home', but are necessary for keeping out draughts from windows and doors, and for keeping everyone warm at night.

When societies became more established and

there was money and time available, the quilting circle would make quilts to commemorate certain events, and together produce really large quilts that would adorn the walls of the buildings that served as community centers.

And of course, the social network was invaluable. The older women would pass on their skills as needlewomen, and designers of quilts and other crafts. More importantly, they would pass on the invaluable knowledge about family life. Childbirth, medicines for common ailments, cooking and how to grow herbs and vegetables – this was the sub-text, and the very important function of the quilting circle.

Clearly in different times, and different places, the women would have different topics that would dominate the quilting circles' conversations.

The quilting circle was common place. It was necessary, it was helpful and social, and it produced wonderful pieces of work for individuals and for communities.

These days, many women live in relative social isolation. Perhaps more so within the much more heavily populated urban environments where most of us live.

Maybe we should rekindle the spark – and start new quilting circles – everywhere!!

Chapter One

The History of Quilting Hawaii

Hawaiian quilting is said to have started when the wives of two chiefs were introduced to quilting by missionaries on board a boat. Hawaiians would not naturally have begun to quilt for domestic use, as quilts were not needed in the warm Hawaiian climate.

The missionaries showed the Hawaiians how to cut up fabrics into pieces and then sew them back together. This the Hawaiians found rather wasteful, as they were careful with all their resources and didn't understand the concept of cutting up a large piece of material, only to sew pieces of it back together, and then be left with bits that couldn't be used.

Eventually, the Hawaiians found a way of using their own clothing fabric (called tapa) which they folded to achieve 1/4 or 1/8 patterns, and they gave any waste pieces back to the missionaries for them to use in their own quilting. This tapa was from tree bark.

The unique nature of the Hawaiian quilting is clear in their use of local flora, and the spirit world as design influences for their quilts. Conceptually, they used quilts to record their environment, their departed love ones, and their still to be born. Their quilts were also strongly about the Hawaiian identity and the identity of the individual members of their society.

The Hawaiian Gods, their rites and ceremonies, and their history, are all depicted in the wonderful Hawaiian quilts. Local events and major historical events were all beautifully detailed and preserved in their quilts. In fact, all their quilts have a story to tell, or a person to describe, or an act to preserve for posterity.

Quilts were not made in Hawaii just to keep the women busy or as a necessary domestic duty. Quilts in Hawaii are their history, and they predict the future too!

One of the few nations to produce famous quilts that were never intended to keep them warm at night, the Hawaiian culture and history has instead been retained beautifully. Quilts continue to be made in Hawaii, with new designs constantly emerging. Here, quilts are both the history and the future in a very unique and valuable way.

The United Kingdom

Clearly a colder climate than Hawaii, the traditions of 'make do and mend' were such that for centuries, cloth was very valuable and not to be wasted. Long before any mechanical cloth production, every piece of cloth was made by hand or with simple weaving frames. Anything so time consuming to produce could only be treated with care and considered to be of value.

Long before the first settlers arrived in America, British women, and men were involved in patchwork and quilting, both for home and commercial benefit. So the history of quilting in Britain goes way back.

There are records of padded clothing being made for soldiers to be worn underneath their armor to protect them from the metal, and also to provide warmth and comfort. And as far back as the fourteenth century, quilted fabrics were used as bedcovers and clothes.

There are examples of eighteenth century pieces of clothing that remain from noble and royal households. For example, an underskirt for a Scottish wedding is now part of the

Heritage Collection of the Quilters Guild, and dated at 1764.

Although in the households run by nobles and royals, there were wonderful examples of luxurious and exquisite pieces of quilting, these were the minority. The very wealthy would import cloth from abroad and use it to display their wealth and social status.

Hence we see silks, satins, velvets, and printed Indian calico used in complex quilting, often as backgrounds to embroidered hangings and bed drapes.

These pieces would generally be made by professional craftsmen who would have been members of some of the early Guilds. Women would not generally have been employed on a commercial basis in this way until much later.

In the homes of the less well off, the quilting and patchwork traditions would have a much more utilitarian approach, and although some would be very cleverly designed and executed, the main concern was to provide warmth without too much expense.

The cottage industry was very much part of the northern England and Welsh tradition, and as such, there would be quilters undertaking work on a commission basis, and either selling directly to certain wealthier homes, or through an agent.

In Wales and some parts of England, there were also traveling workers. They would take board and lodging in a household and be required to provide new quilts for bedding, along with other stitch work in exchange for their keep.

In Victorian times, fashion dictated the use of lots of bright colors and contrasting black. Fabrics were more readily available and there was greater wealth available in the new middle classes. Drapery and bed coverings that had previously been seen only in the houses of the nobility were now emulated by the new professional and commercial classes.

Most girls of 'good' homes would be brought up to be competent, at the very least, with their needle and thread. So the practice of embroidery, patchwork, quilting, and appliqué was very much kept alive.

However, by the beginning of the twentieth century and the outbreak of war, things were beginning to change.

When war broke out, women found they had to work to help the war effort. This meant little time for hobbies, and rationing meant that everyone concentrated on getting enough food to feed the family and getting the domestic necessities. There was little time or energy for needlework as a hobby.

By the end of the 1940's, things had begun to back to normal, the country was becoming more and more reliant on manufactured clothes and bedding. Factories had sprung up across the UK, and imports began subsequently to add to the large amount of manufactured goods.

Really it was the resurgence of quilting arising from the United States that helped Britain resurrects its quilting traditions. Now the Quilters Guild has a valuable role in supporting quilting in the UK. The Guild set up a British Quilting Study Group in 1998, and this provides invaluable support to the quilters of today with research and information.

British quilting has, however, never managed to equal the art of the American quilting traditions, and America has been entirely responsible for spreading the word and the work of quilting across the world as far as Australia, Japan, South Africa and Europe.

Were it not for America, the UK may have allowed its quilting history to fade away. Thankfully, however, it has helped to revive quilting both as a hobby and as an art form.

Australian Quilting

Women were given the materials and tools to make patch work quilts en route to their Australian destination so that they could sell them and be able to support themselves when they landed.

Sadly, only one of these appears to have survived, but it is clear that the British women brought with them the skills and traditions of quilting.

Quilting was thought to be a 'suitable' occupation for a lady, and the quilters soon began to put their work together at exhibitions, and a market in quilts was quickly established. The British traditions were retained, and quilting in Australia continues to respect and reflect the styles and patterns of the mother country.

However, for many years, Australian families were very poor, and generally the women were responsible for 'making' all the bedding, as well as all the clothes and household fabrics. In the absence of money to buy good cloth, the women used their initiative. They used old sacks, old grain bags and anything that could be used to give warmth. With luck, they would be able to find or get something to make a bed cover more attractive, and the sacks would be used as the wadding or batting. Old cloth would be cut and stitched either directly onto the batting, or as a face fabric, and whatever artistic talent the maker had would be used.

Later on it became commonplace to obtain old sample books from traveling salesmen. So many quilts were made with suit cloth, as well as old curtains, and what ever else was available.

Sadly, these days Australian women tend to be too busy to do a great deal of quilting. And of course, with the much more cheaply available goods, it's now a time of buy new and throws away the old. Not like the old days, which epitomized the make do and mend motto.

Japanese quilting is renowned for the strong religious and spiritual influences. Quilts were highly valued and given as markers of respect to the emperors and ruling warriors. The recipient of a quilt is being wished a long life, and the giving of quilting fabric is imbued with spiritual significance.

The Japanese have traditionally worn quilted garments, particularly jackets and house gowns. The most famous are the Yosegire patch work quilts from the 16th Century, which are made using fabric strips. These are still made and worn today, and provide both warmth and luxury. Now Japanese quilts have wonderful appliqué and embroidery, and have continued to be considered of great importance.

The French Tradition

As with the United Kingdom, the recent resurgence of interest in quilting is really a consequence of the way the American craft industry has captured the world since the 1960's.

Although in a domestic sphere, there has always been quilting and needlework in France, this had largely been lost as an art form. The holding of a major exhibition in the 1970's, which captured the imagination of many Parisians, and the opening of a quilting and patchwork shop in the center of Paris was the beginning of a new life for quilting in France.

Over the last thirty years, quilting has blossomed in France, and from being an obscure hobby, with materials and tools being hard to find, it has become an increasingly substantial business.

The design of quilts in France is, as you would imagine, of major importance. Both traditional and contemporary designs are very popular now. Small and very intricately worked pieces have a particular beauty and are highly regarded.

The appliqué work, particularly the Baltimore style, and the patchwork form are really the most popular here.

The matelessage type of quilting is really popular. This uses a whole piece of fabric with the quilting lines drawn on, and then put together with a plain backing piece and central padding, and held taut on a frame for the stitching.

The top fabric might be silk or finely woven and printed cotton. The design markings are followed with a simple running stitch, but very finely sewn. The patterns are simple taken one by one, but the pieces are very densely sewn so the end product is a very rich and heavily worked.

These make wonderful bed coverings, and the style is used for cheaper manufactured pieces which have now gained a huge market across Europe.

There is a major annual festival, now in its 10th year, which succeeds in enticing over 17,000 people from all over the world. Over 800 quilts were exhibited at the most recent show, so you can see how seriously the French are now taking quilting!

The Piquré de Marseilles is also very famous, and was made from two pieces of fabric, and a back cloth and a fine silk or cotton front piece. The pattern was worked with back stitch, and the filling was inserted between the needle holes. The patterns are not dissimilar to those of William Morris, famous for his Arts and Craft Movement in the United Kingdom.

The method was amended later on for ease of working, and running stitch used instead of backstitch, and more padding used to fill out the areas between the patterns. The stitching work is generally done in a contrasting color to the face fabric, and this type of quilting makes wonderful cushions and items of clothing, such as evening jackets.

The boutis evolved to show increasingly larger areas of pattern which could be done much faster. The name of this type of quilting comes from the Provencal for stuffing. The

Provencal style was also part of this tradition, and local flora and fauna, as well as religious and romantic designs, were used, reflecting the interests and feelings of the young women quilters.

Later on, predominantly white cotton was used, and these beautiful pieces are famous for being as wonderful on the back of the fabric as on the face. The plain white bed covers, pillow covers and throws are sought after, and similar styles found in many shops like Laura Ashley in the United Kingdom. The style was also used for baby clothes and cot covers. The style, although without the padding, has also become a classic for good quality underwear.

Sadly, this style of work is less common these days, but fashion trends can always surprise, and it may be that it is making a comeback.

Although it's known as a French Provencal style, it does apparently originate in Sicily at some point during the Middle Ages.

South African quilts

With a warm climate, you would not imagine quilts being necessary to keep warm. However, they are used to depict the history and the culture of South Africa.

There is, for example, a quilt made by Phina Nkosi, who works with the Zamani Quilting Sisters in Soweto. This group formed to try and help women who not only had to live in a racist society, but also a very sexist one. This group worked on the principle of self help, and established a women's resource center. This quilt includes portraits of women she believed were part of the struggle for freedom in South Africa. The quilt is hung in the MSU Museum Accession, and was bought in conjunction with the South African Cultural Heritage Project. This museum has an extensive collection of quilts, and you can obtain more information by visiting their web site at:

museum.msu.edu/s%2Dprogram/mtap/Collections/sata.html

The United States of America and Canada

Perhaps the most well known quilting is from this region of the world. In the northern states and Canada, quilting has been part of a very strong tradition in domestic arts and crafts, ensuring American and Canadian families had both beautiful and functional fabrics in their homes.

However, it is most definitely the stuff of myth and legend that quilting was commonplace, either for practical or decorative reasons, in the early colonial times.

The original settlers worked hard and long, and there was little time spare for the artistic quilting that we mistakenly link to these early days. In these days, plain cloth and wadding would have been used to reflect the restrictive religious beliefs of many of the settlers for whom decoration was considered inappropriate.

These early colonial women would have to weave their own cloth, and undertake all the other domestic tasks – and apart from the fact that the men were considered above such humble work, they tended to be outside in the fields, tending the big livestock, and building or fencing.

Women's lives were hard, and initially often lonely. They had poor access to civilization, often settling in isolated areas, with near neighbors possibly miles away.

Only later on, as families and farms became more established, and the community facilities developed, were women able to have the time and leisure to quilt. Even then it was largely in the better off homes where domestic help was brought in, that the lady of the house would do the decorative quilting.

Of course, women settlers would bring with them the skills learned from their families, so a variety of styles and patterns were imported via them to America. Nevertheless, there was only a very limited amount of fabric available in the early days, and it wasn't really until the mid 1800's that there was fabric available for quilting to be affordable. Prior to this date, most families used blankets – of varying quality and warmth, but nevertheless cheaper than quilts.

The colonial style underwent resurgence in the twentieth century. The styles of houses, of furniture, and the soft furnishings, all became very popular, both in America, and abroad. The idea of 'old colonial style quilts' was part of the marketing done by magazines and manufacturers, but the quilts they were advertising were definitely made much later than they suggested, probably from the 1850s.

About this time, the manufacturing industry

was becoming established, and women in America found they could buy materials. Those who had sheep for wool and grew cotton, could get the raw materials made up into fabric, and no longer had the hard, and time consuming job of weaving and fabric making.

This gave women more time for other things, among them of course, was quilting. So this is really the point in time where American quilt making really became a reality.

Patterns became available, and could be bought in magazines or in stores, but American women enjoyed using the patterns that their friends and family used, and pattern sharing was the norm, rather than buying new ones. These patterns became the traditional American quilting patterns that are still famous today.

Quilting was not an easy hobby for many women. Space in the homes of the majority was limited. The quilting frames were generally large enough for at least 6 women to work at, and initially were home made.

Most homes didn't have spare space for the frame, so it would both be put together and then taken apart as needed, or connected to a pulley system and hoisted up to the ceiling when not being used.

The quilting bees that enabled women to get together were limited to the number of people who could fit in the available space around the frame.

Chapter Two

The Technical Bits

There are different styles of quilting, which largely reflect the country of origin and traditions of their quilting history.

Effectively though, quilting requires a sandwich of fabrics. You begin with a face fabric, which can be made up of patchwork or blocks, or which could be a plain color, or a printed fabric.

The padding, or batting, used to be inserted between the stitched areas in some old quilted pieces, such as quilt surrounds for wall hangings that were principally works of high quality embroidery.

However, these days, and particularly for bed cover quilts, there are three layers. The top layer, which if it is patchwork will have been made up separately of small pieces of fabric joined together to make blocks or sections. The blocks or sections are then stitched together. When the size or overall design has been achieved, this is then put together with the batting and a back fabric, and the quilt is created by stitching the three layers together. This should really be described as a patchwork quilt.

However, there are lots of other sorts of quilts.

If the face fabric tells a story, it is unlikely that the base fabric will be decorated. The stitching is probably going to be on the outlines of the figures, emblems or picture elements of the fabric.

Or, plain fabric can be beautifully decorated using only stitching to create pattern, figures, flowers or whatever you like.

If, however, you are creating a bed cover, or drape, you may want to use the stitching to create the pattern on both face and base fabrics.

Machine quilting is now very popular, as it clearly enables quilters to produce work faster than by hand. However, depending on the type of quilt you are making, it can be difficult to handle, or it might not give the effect that you want.

Hand quilting is still a very popular method for many, as it does give a softer, and perhaps more luxurious look. Again, depending on the size, you may need a hoop which will secure a section of the quilt, or if it's a bed cover, you may really need a frame to stretch out a larger area of the quilt.

The old ones were hand made to suit the

space available and the number of people who could work on the piece at any one time. You can still make your own. Use timber lengths covered in fabric so that you can pin your quilt to the fabric and hold it in place. The ends can be used to roll the fabric forwards and backwards so that only the working area is stretched out.

If you are doing hand quilting, you will need quilting needles and quilting thread. Traditionally, you sew with one hand, and use the other hand underneath to guide the needle back through to the face. The key is to keep the stitches the same length and absolutely in line. They don't have to be minute, but they do have to all be identical to give a good finish.

You can use different colored threads to match the color of the fabric, or contrasting colors, or even colorless thread.

If you are using a sewing machine, a walking foot will ensure all three layers of the quilt move together – it's important not to allow one part of the sandwich to be more out of sync with the others.

Some of the terminology for quilting that you will find useful is given below:

Accent quilting can add pattern that works with, but follows, different lines to those of any patchwork.

Achromatic color schemes - using black white and grey only

Album quilts – these use a mix of blocks pertinent to the maker, the recipient or an event, and are usually gifts for specific events or circumstances

Amish Quilts – these are very simplistic and orderly and always functional

Analogous color schemes – neighboring colors on a color wheel

Anchor fabric – this is used when piecing to hold the fabric pieces together when machine piecing

Appliqué – not specific to quilting, but often used on quilts – this is the use of smaller pieces of fabric, often making a figure or character, stitched to the face fabric of the quilt. Sun Bonnett Sue's are examples of these. Various stitches can be used – visible or invisible

Backing fabric – as you would expect, this is this is the base fabric

Bargello quilting – use of fabric strips to give the look of a wave

Basting is a way of holding the three sandwich layers together on a temporary basis. You can tack, pin or use sticky spray

Batting is the middle or wadding layer of your quilt sandwich

Bearding is when the batting fibers come away and find their way through to the face or base fabric – it happens more with polyester wadding.

Beaswax coating on thread makes it stronger

and prevents it from knotting.

Betweens are quilting needles, and they are very short. Sizes 9, 10 or 12 are generally used – the 12 being longer than the nine.

Binding is used to create the quilt edges. It is essential to cut binding on the bias to avoid pulling out of shape.

Blanket stitch – originally used to edge blankets and prevent fraying, it is also used as a decorative stitch for securing pieces of appliqué

Block – a section of patchwork, usually, but not always, square

Border – fabric strips used between blocks and or on the top bottom and sides.

Cats ears – a block style also known as prairie points

Chain sewing- a continual thread to sew pieces together without finishing off and restarting

Chain stitch – is an embroidery stitch that resembles a chain.

Charm quilts have only one shape which is used repeatedly, but never using the same fabric more than once

Cheaters Cloth – fabric which looks like it is made of patchwork, but which is actually printed

Cool colours – blues or greens

Crazy quilt – quilt using irregular fabric pieces stitched to foundation fabric and then decorated.

Cross hatch – parallel lines marked on the quilt to help hand stitching.

Cross hatching uses straight lines on a grid – diamonds or square or rectangles can be used.

Dimensional appliqué – this stands in relief

from the quilt cover, either stuffed or not.

Echo quilting – lines of quilting that repeat around the edge of a piece or design

Fat Quarter is a yard and a half of fabric cut in half to enable a square piece 18" x 22"

Foundation blocks are blocks that are made up of any number of small pieces of fabric. The finished block is then joined to other finished blocks to create the patchwork face. Try and keep the fabric, if possible, to have the straight grain on the edge of the block.

Frames can be small circular hoops for hand sewing or large rectangular frames for holding bigger quilts.

Friendship quilt – made to be given to friends or family and often having messages or using swap fabric

Grain – the line of fiber running perpendicular to the side selvedge

Hawaiian appliqué – A technique for applying very detailed design pieces onto quilt fabric.

Hoops – large frames to hold the quilt for hand or machine stitching

Lap quilting – quilting squares as complete pieces, and then joining the pieces when they are all made

Lattice strips – strips bordering the blocks

Loft – the spare between face and the backing fabrics – high lofts mean warmer, thicker quilts

Meandering or stippling style – this is a style of filling in areas of quilt with stitch, but none of the stitching should touch. So you can't cross over a line you have already stitched

Marking – marking the quilt by tracing or freehand to indicate where to stitch the quilt. Tailors chalk or wax is often used – soap also works.

Medallion quilt – a quilt with a central design from which the rest of the design follows outwards

Millennium quilts - or Y2K quilts – to commemorate the year 2000

Miters – a method of measuring diagonals and angles

Monochromatic – all one color

Motif stitching gives a pattern which can be done on plain or patch work quilting. Motifs allow the quilter to incorporate names, hearts, animals, flowers, in fact any object, or, an abstract pattern.

Muslin – a very thin plain fabric, often used as a foundation fabric for piecing blocks

No knots – No knots are to be seen when quilting. The trick is to pull the knot through to the batting layer so that it can be hidden. When you finish you will also need to lose your knot in the centre batting. As with a starter knot, wrap the cotton a couple of times round the needle, check your last stitch hole, and pop the needle back in, and pull it through so that the knot stops in the batting, then cut the thread close to the fabric.

Off hand – usually the left hand which guides the needle from underneath the quilt

Outline stitching is, as you would expect, intended to provide an outline, and achieved by stitching about ¼ away from the seam. By doing this, the quilt is strengthened, as you get, in effect, a double line of stitching, and the other advantage is that the stitching is inside the cut edge and no seal allowance is needed.

Paper piecing – using paper to attach pieces in a block. The paper is usually numbered or lettered and the pieces are matched, stitched to the paper and the adjoining pieces.

Piecing – stitching pieces of fabric together – or called patchwork

Quilting Thread is single strand of very strong cotton and glazed to help it pass through the batting.

Rocking – this is the popular method – if you rock the needle back and forth you should be able to get about 4 or 5 stitches on at one go.

Sampler – showing a number of different quilting techniques

Sashing – fabric strips that separate blocks

Satin Stich – side by side stitching

Selvedge – the edges of the fabric where the weave was finished.

Seminole quilting – creating large pieces of fabric with pieces so that the joined fabric can then be cut and used with shapes repeated.

Sewing in the ditch refers to stitching very close to a seam where the stitches are barely visible.

Sharps – fine needles for joining pieces and stitching on appliqué

Stencil – using a pre made shape for transferring designs and motifs

Template – a shape for cutting pieces – made of plastic, paper, sandpaper.

Warm colors – orange, red, yellows and tans

Piecing together the foundation blocks is easiest using foundation paper. This will need to be marked so that you can attach the fabric matching your number sequence. Each piece needs to be sewn both to the paper and together. Small stitches (min. 14 per inch) and machine needle size 14 is recommended.

Experts recommend using tracing paper for machine stitching, but not for hand stitching. Other options are the paper used in medical exam rooms – it's cheap, and works very well. Anther option is the vegetable parchment you use in the kitchen, which some people find works very well. The tracing paper will pull away really easily after you have created your block, as long as you use small stitches. Muslin is recommended for hand piecing.

Present the wrong side of the fabric to the central piece to the back of the foundation paper ensuring you have a quarter inch seam allowance all round. Machine the paper and fabric together.

Then take a piece of fabric for an adjoining section, and place the right side of the fabric facing the right side of the first piece. Then turn over the foundation paper to see the marked side, and sew on the line between shown between the first and second piece. Then when you turn it over, the second piece should cover its space with the necessary seam allowance.

Next, lay the work down with the numbers on the foundation paper facing you. Fold the paper on the stitching line you have just done, so that the numbers on the paper face each other and the seam allowance of the first piece and the main fabric of the second piece are open. Cut the fabric to the minimum of a quarter inch on the edges.

Patterns can be made from almost anything. The traditional American patterns work on a block or section, and are repeated throughout the quilt, with each block being made up of a number of pieces. The quilts are then edged to surround the blocks.

Traditionally, paper and sand paper have been used. The benefit of sandpaper is the fabric will stick to it well and not slide. Now you can find plastic template material that has a much longer life than paper, and doesn't blunt the scissors like sand paper, nor does it catch on anything.

So how do you make the patterns for quilting?

First, of course, it depends on why you are making a quilt, which determines what sort of pattern you would like and what sort of fabrics you would use.

For patchwork quilting – most American Colonial Style for example, it's very straight forward to make your patterns, and you can find lots of examples, with sizes, for you to print off from the internet.

Cut paper templates for your shapes, and

then trace them on to sand paper (fine gauge) or plastic template material. Then trace the templates onto the fabric and cut out.

Or, if you are making a quilt from varying shaped pieces, you can make a large paper or card design, and gradually cut out and put together sections to match your design.

You will need to determine the sequence of stitching to create each square or section if there are overlapping pieces of fabric. Follow the tips above for using foundation paper, which is numbered to reflect the pieces you use to make up the block.

The art of quilting is really in the care and precision, both in the planning stage, and for the stitching.

These days you can buy wadding to sit between the back and face fabrics, and stitch through to create the quilt finish. If you secure the three sections, i.e., the back cloth, the wadding, and the face fabric at strategic points, you can then appliqué the decorative pattern on the face fabric.

Rotary cutting is more precise than using scissors. The cutters are extremely sharp, and need to be used with care – definitely something to be kept out of sight and access for youngsters.

When you use a rotary cutter you need a proper cutting mat that won't get ridged from the blade and won't damage the blade either. If you use a damaged mat, the cutter can slide off course, which could mean that your fabric wouldn't have the straight edge you need. The cutters should always have their blades closed when not in use, and the guard in place whenever you are not using it.

Even experienced quilters and crafts people have managed to cut themselves, so it is essential to ensure you have the right mat, that the cutter blade is only open when you are actually using it, and that blade and mat are kept clear of bits and pieces. Do take care when using the cutter, and don't allow your attention to wander or you risk cutting yourself, and worse – getting blood on your lovely quilting fabric.

Most people working with soft furnishings of all descriptions have an iron and ironing surface in their work space. Pressing fabric to create your seam lines makes assembling pieces and blocks that much easier. Having said that, many people do prefer to finger press the edges of the smaller pieces, and when all is said and done, it is personal preference and skill level that informs your decision.

However, for rotary cutting, when you need to create the cross fabric line for cutting, it does make it much easier if you use the iron. Before you cut the cross line, fold the material selvedge edge to selvedge edge and ensure the material lies smooth with the grain of the material in the fold. Then fold it again so the first fold and the two selvedge edges are aligned.

Machine stitching large quilts can be quite tricky. If you don't have a massive work table that will hold the complete quilt, try putting together some pasting tables, or support some board on chairs. You will find it much easier to work if the quilt is not catching on the edge of your work table and being weighted down.

You can find a host of information on 'how to' with quilting, in books, on the internet and in craft magazines. However it's much more fun to find someone who has a level of expertise, and volunteer to work with them on one of their own quilts – you gain experience, and hopefully friendship.

Chapter Three

Quilt Decorating

Appliqué is a really decorative medium that allows your artistic skills full scope. It's a lovely way to incorporate personal, or any detail really, and it's possible to do something really very simple, or really very complex and highly worked.

Some of the very popular American styles are called 'sun bonnet Sue' Basically, they consist of a bonnet, a triangular shaped dress with curved bottom hem, an arm, and a foot – and of course any ancillary figures you like – umbrella, duck, dog, kitten, etc. You can use any mix of fabrics, and you can decorate the fabrics with stitching for details, like buttons, shoe laces, dress or bonnet trims etc.

These are wonderful for bed covers and wall hangings in little girls' bedrooms, cot covers, bed covers etc.

There are lots of ways of using appliqué, and they are all correct! The only wrong way, is a way you don't feel comfortable with.

You can create your whole figure first and then either tuck in the edges as you go – a toothpick or large darning needle both work well – and use whichever stitch you prefer. On some pieces, blanket stitch will look just right, and on others you won't want to see any stitching so you can use a hemming catch stitch or running stitch.

Appliqué is a great way to make smaller wall hangings, where you want to create a picture. Let's say you want to have some simple flowers on a relatively plain background. Choose the fabrics you want, whether they are contrasting or complementary, and draw out your design. Decide whether you want any embroidery, or whether you want to create a mix of fabric as the back ground. Then create your appliqué pieces, padded and backed if required, but not if you prefer not, and then secure them to your background quilt.

Of course you can use appliqué on all sorts of things, and not just on quilts.

And you can buy ready made motifs if you wish, and use these to decorate plain quilts, or even to hide any damage. There are lots of patterns available on the internet or in mail order catalogues.

You can mix and match with appliqué and collage — so some pieces are invisibly stitched others can be clearly in relief, with edges, ng ribbons, whatever works with your .gn.

The main thing is not to be scared of having a go — you can assemble most of your appliqué or collage before fixing to your quilt — its great fun and really not difficult.

Using painted or batik colored fabric for quilts is great fun too.

Another great way of incorporating your individual ideas and designs into quilts is to use fabric that you have hand painted o treated in the batik style. You can use th color lines as stitching lines, or combi stitch patterns with color lines as you wish.

Trawl the internet, visit your local museums, look at paintings or de anywhere and everywhere.

You will find hundreds of thousands o about what you might like your quilts like – or ideas that help you create your own unique design.

You can use paint, ribbon, all sorts of dress making or furnishing store items, motifs, embroidery pieces – embroidery faces even, absolutely anything.

Chapter Four

Unique and Important Quilts Across The World

...e some very famous and very ...quilts that are notable and are part ... – whether that is ancient or

...cent is the 'Remembrance ...the September 11th attacks ...s was made by first and ...n from Roy Gomm ...his is a very patriotic

You can mix and match with appliqué and collage – so some pieces are invisibly stitched and others can be clearly in relief, with edges, trailing ribbons, whatever works with your design.

The main thing is not to be scared of having a go – you can assemble most of your appliqué or collage before fixing to your quilt – its great fun and really not difficult.

Using painted or batik colored fabric for quilts is great fun too.

Another great way of incorporating your individual ideas and designs into quilts is to use fabric that you have hand painted or treated in the batik style. You can use the color lines as stitching lines, or combine stitch patterns with color lines as you wish.

Trawl the internet, visit your local craft museums, look at paintings or designs anywhere and everywhere.

You will find hundreds of thousands of ideas about what you might like your quilts to look like – or ideas that help you create your own unique design.

You can use paint, ribbon, all sorts of dress making or furnishing store items, motifs, embroidery pieces – embroidery faces even, absolutely anything.

Chapter Four

Unique and Important Quilts

Across The World

There are some very famous and very important quilts that are notable and are part of history – whether that is ancient or contemporary.

Of the more recent is the 'Remembrance Quilt', made after the September 11th attacks in New York. This was made by first and sixth grade children from Roy Gomm Elementary School. This is a very patriotic quilt, designed to show the flag, and indicates the invaluable support from volunteers in the Red Cross that made recovery from the September 11th possible.

The Red Cross quilts are very famous and have been used as a fund raising method for years.

The Red Cross had already got a really famous quilt in its 'Signature Quilt'. This isn't, however, just one quilt – it is the name given to quilts produced for fundraising, as a means of providing therapy and a way of expressing the commitment of the many people involved in their making.

It's astonishing that the simple Red Cross emblem can be reproduced so many different ways and provide such a valuable means of support to the volunteer movement.

The Red Cross Signature Quilts were first made in 1918 to raise funds for the war effort. It established the tradition of incorporating the values of volunteer work and community, bravery and care of the injured and sick. This first quilt was signed by President Woodrow Wilson and his wife, Theodore Roosevelt, Helen Keller and Sarah Bernhardt amongst others.

The Guicciardini Coverlet is reputedly the oldest quilt in the world and has been dated to the 1300s. Half of it is housed in the Victoria and Albert Museum in London, and the other half housed in Florence, this is very valuable and carefully guarded.

The oldest quilting museum is said to be the San Jose Museum of Quilts and Textiles in California. This museum has ever changing exhibitions, and examples of some of the finest quilting from Hawaii and the Amish and Shaker communities in America.

This is a wonderful display of both the very traditional and the very modern pattern styles, and is well worth a visit.

In Australia, in the Eskbank House and

Museum Collection, there is a quilt dating back to 1893 known as The Sutton Family Crazy Patchwork Quilt, but the actual maker is not known. This is one of the earliest examples of Australian patchwork quilting.

There is a quilt made by Mary Mayne depicting real places in a village called Eaton Bray in the United Kingdom – it's a wonderful way of preserving information for future generations. Mary is also a member of the American Quilting Guild.

Mary Mayne also made the Winston Churchill quilt that is displayed at Bletchley Park when the Enigma Code was broken during the war.

These are examples of the ways quilts can reflect the lives of real people, real events, and real places.

Chapter Five

Quilts – Births, Marriages and Deaths

Quilts have been used from birth to death – to celebrate, to mark life changes, for the holding of memories, and to mourn.

Quilts for babies' cribs are almost a necessity. If you don't make one for your own baby, an aunt, grandmother, cousin or friend is likely to make one for you.

The advantage of crib quilts is their size – easier to work with, not so time consuming – and an excuse to really go to town with design and skill for a newborn.

Quilts in America were often made to signify an engagement to be married. Creating quilts for the newlyweds' home was always a joyful undertaking, and a chance for the girls to get together, for advice to be given, and the lucky girl to let the world know how happy she was.

Wedding presents – what better than a quilt. They are markers of your children's lives and their path into the future with families of their own.

There are many very fortunate children who

have quilts made for them by their grandmothers. Incorporating references to the child hood life and family, pets, friends, and places they have lived and visited. These are irreplaceable and beyond value, and I wish I had had one made for me!

Sadly too, in death – in the American civil war, soldiers were often buried in their quilts, which they had taken with them to keep them warm at night. Many quilts were, of course, destroyed during the war, and many were taken as mementos by others.

Quilts were made after death too, as commemoratives of the departed, and to indicate the grief and sadness of the mourners.

Perhaps more than any other of household linen, the quilt has a from birth to death, and can be as al or impersonal, as cheerful or sad, small, colorful, patterned or plain. ber of

They can be decorated in

ways, and using almost any sort of fabric, the quilt is both an exceedingly practical and potentially stunningly beautiful piece. It is a combination of traditional or modern styles, personal choice, lovingly sewn and an indicator of our self, our place and our time.

Fashions apply in the world of quilting as with other textiles. We have seen the resurgence, in particular, of the traditional patterns of American patch work, and these are really now considered classic styles, and hopefully will continue forever.

The joy of quilting, however, is in its variety, and its potential for the artistic talent of the creator. The large and complex patchwork patterns are wonderful, and just as wonderful are smaller quilts, which can say anything you want.

They can be about your family, your home, your village, city or country.

They can be about your joys or your sorrow; your love or your loss.

have quilts made for them by their grandmothers. Incorporating references to the child hood life and family, pets, friends, and places they have lived and visited. These are irreplaceable and beyond value, and I wish I had had one made for me!

Sadly too, in death – in the American civil war, soldiers were often buried in their quilts, which they had taken with them to keep them warm at night. Many quilts were, of course, destroyed during the war, and many were taken as mementos by others.

Quilts were made after death too, as commemoratives of the departed, and to indicate the grief and sadness of the mourners.

Perhaps more than any other piece of household linen, the quilt has a role from birth to death, and can be as personal or impersonal, as cheerful or sad, large or small, colorful, patterned or plain.

They can be decorated in any number of

ways, and using almost any sort of fabric, the quilt is both an exceedingly practical and potentially stunningly beautiful piece. It is a combination of traditional or modern styles, personal choice, lovingly sewn and an indicator of our self, our place and our time.

Fashions apply in the world of quilting as with other textiles. We have seen the resurgence, in particular, of the traditional patterns of American patch work, and these are really now considered classic styles, and hopefully will continue forever.

The joy of quilting, however, is in its variety, and its potential for the artistic talent of the creator. The large and complex patchwork patterns are wonderful, and just as wonderful are the smaller quilts, which can say anything you want.

- They can be about your family, your home, your village, city or country.
- They can be about your joys or your despair; your love or your loss.

In California, for example, there is The Quilt Project, which is part of the Cervical Cancer program, and which has squares made in memory of women who have lost their lives to the cancer, or who have suffered cancer but have been fortunate enough to beat it.

There are also quilts put together to hold the memories of people who have died from Aids or Ovarian Cancer.

They are all beautiful pieces of work, and wonderful works of art. They are also very personal to the people who have lost loved ones, and commemorate the people who died or suffered.

The quilts are exhibited in health centers, hospitals and doctors' surgeries, and are used to raise awareness, to raise funding and to help promote more research.

Conclusion

Quilting has a long history, and it would seem a good long future. The traditions of the early quilters have not been lost, and they have been taken all over the world. The British women took their skills and traditions to the other side of the world, to America and to Australia. American quilters in the twentieth century are responsible for bringing this craft into the twenty first century – all over the world.

The Hawaiian people record their history through their quilts, and show the world their spiritual and religious past and present.

The French have used quilting as a medium for their artistic drive, and have produced some of the most beautiful quilts, with intricate and artistic stitching.

Japanese clothing has traditionally included quilt work, and the wonderful silks of the kimono can be fabulously luxurious when appliquéd and quilted.

South Africa, too, has strong love affair with

quilting, and the colors and patterns reflect the climate, its colors and its wild life.

There are quilts across the world that have remained in the same family for generations, and there are quilts displayed in museums and exhibitions, in town halls, in hotels, in company offices and in restaurants.

There are ancient quilts that can now be purchased so that their stories and makers can live on. And of course, there are all the quilts yet to be made!

Quilting can be simple or complex patchwork; it can be the most exquisite stitchery on simple or costly fabrics. You can quilt a small cushion cover, a bed cover, a jacket, a handbag, a small medium or huge wall hanging. You can use painted or dyed fabrics, and you can add motifs, appliqués or incorporate ribbons, pearls or diamonds.

There is almost any style, any size, any use, as long as it's a quilt.

Quilting Book for Beginners